SOUPS

BRIMAR

Editor Angela Rahaniotis
Graphic Design Zapp
Photography Marc Bruneau
Food Preparation / Stylist Josée Robitaille
Assistant Stylist Marc Maula
Tableware courtesy of Stokes

© 1995 Brimar Publishing Inc.
338 Saint Antoine St. East
Montreal, Canada H2Y 1A3
Tel.: (514) 954-1441
Fax: (514) 954-5086

ISBN 2-89433-124-X
Printed in Canada

SOUPS

There is nothing like the aroma
of a big pot of homemade soup
to tantalize the appetite.
And this book has soups for every
occasion, whether you are looking for
a hearty and nourishing main course,
a light and delicious starter, or a chilled
creation for those hot days when eating
a heavy meal holds no appeal.

Soup making used to be considered
a finicky and time-consuming procedure,
but the food processor has changed
all that. With a food processor,
you can chop your ingredients quickly,
or purée a creamy soup in almost no time.

Many soups taste even better the next
day, so don't hesitate to make more
than you need for one meal.

Finally, don't forget to use these recipes
as the inspiration for your own creations.
Soup making is one of the most practical
and interesting ways to use up those bits
and pieces of vegetables and meat
in your refrigerator.

Vegetables

CELERIAC

BEETS

CARROTS

LEEKS

RUTABAGA

TURNIPS

RED CABBAGE

BRUSSELS SPROUTS

CAULIFLOWER

WHITE
CABBAGE

SAVOY CABBAGE

BROCCOLI

SNOW PEAS

MUSHROOMS

ZUCCHINI

SPINACH

ASPARAGUS

FENNEL

AVOCADO

CELERY

OKRA

PEPPERS

Herbs

TARRAGON

BASIL

PARSLEY

CHIVES

CORIANDER

OREGANO

THYME

BAY LEAVES

MARJORAM

DILL

ROSEMARY

SAGE

CHERVIL

SORREL

Homemade Chicken Stock

2	leeks, white part only	2
4 lb	cleaned chicken, fat trimmed	1.8 kg
16 cups	cold water	4 L
4	carrots, pared	4
2	celery stalks, cut in two	2
2	onions, quartered, unpeeled	2
½	small turnip, peeled and cubed	½
2	sprigs fresh parsley	2
1	sprig fresh thyme	1
1 tbsp	basil	15 mL
2	bay leaves	2
1	clove	1
1 tsp	rosemary	5 mL
	salt and pepper	

1 Slit leeks from top to bottom twice, leaving 1 in (2.5 cm) intact at base. Wash leeks under cold, running water to remove dirt and sand.

2 Place chicken in large pot and add water. Bring to boil and cook 2 minutes; skim liquid.

3 Add vegetables. Place fresh herbs and seasonings in piece of cheesecloth and secure with string. Add to liquid. Cook 1½ hours over low heat.

4 Remove chicken from pot and reserve for other uses. Turn off heat under pot. Add 1 cup (250 mL) of cold water to liquid in pot. Let stand 6 minutes.

5 Pass stock through sieve lined with cheesecloth. Refrigerate up to 3 days or freeze up to 3 months.

This white chicken stock is used in a variety of recipes.

Homemade Veal Stock

2	leeks, white part only	2
3 lb	lean veal trimmings	1.4 kg
16 cups	cold water	4 L
2 cups	dry white wine	500 mL
4	carrots, pared	4
2	celery stalks, cut in two	2
2	onions, peeled and studded with cloves	2
2	sprigs fresh parsley	2
2	sprigs fresh basil	2
1	sprig fresh thyme	1
1 tsp	chervil	5 mL
1	bay leaf	1
	salt and pepper	

1 Slit leeks from top to bottom twice, leaving 1 in (2.5 cm) intact at base. Wash leeks under cold, running water to remove dirt and sand.

2 Place meat in large pot and add water. Bring to boil and cook 2 minutes; skim liquid.

3 Add wine and vegetables. Place fresh herbs and seasonings in piece of cheesecloth and secure with string. Add to liquid. Cook 2 hours over low heat.

4 Remove meat. Pass stock through sieve lined with cheese-cloth. Refrigerate up to 3 days or freeze up to 3 months.

This light veal stock is used in a variety of recipes.

Homemade Beef Stock

2	leeks, white part only	2
4 lb	blade steak roast, fat trimmed	1.8 kg
16 cups	cold water	4 L
3	carrots, pared	3
2	celery stalks, cut in two	2
2	onions, quartered, unpeeled	2
½	turnip, peeled and quartered	½
1	sprig fresh thyme	1
2	sprigs fresh parsley	2
2	bay leaves	2
2	cloves	2
1 tbsp	basil	15 mL
	salt and pepper	

1 Slit leeks from top to bottom twice, leaving 1 in (2.5 cm) intact at base. Wash leeks under cold, running water to remove dirt and sand.

2 Place meat in large pot and add water. Bring to boil and cook 2 minutes; skim liquid.

3 Add vegetables. Place fresh herbs and seasonings in piece of cheesecloth and secure with string. Add to liquid. Cook 3 hours over very low heat.

4 Remove meat and reserve for other uses. Add 1 cup (250 mL) cold water to liquid in pot. Simmer 15 minutes.

5 Pass stock through sieve lined with cheesecloth. Refrigerate up to 3 days or freeze up to 3 months.

This dark beef stock is used in a variety of recipes.

Homemade Medium Beef Stock

3 lb	beef chuck	1.4 kg
1	beef marrow bone	1
12 cups	water	3 L
3	sprigs fresh parsley	3
1	sprig fresh thyme	1
1	bay leaf	1
4	carrots, pared	4
1	small turnip, peeled and halved	1
1	large leek, white part only, cleaned	1
2	onions, halved and studded with cloves	2
5	celery leaves	5
	salt and pepper	

1 Place beef and bone in pot and add water. Bring to boil and cook 10 minutes; skim liquid. Transfer beef and bone to clean saucepan. Strain liquid and reserve.

2 Tie fresh herbs and bay leaf together. Place in saucepan and add vegetables and celery leaves. Pour in reserved liquid and season well. Bring to boil. Cook 3 hours over very low heat.

3 Pass liquid through sieve lined with cheesecloth. Refrigerate up to 3 days or freeze up to 3 months.

White Sauce for Cream Soups

¼ cup	butter	50 mL
¼ cup	flour	50 mL
4½ cups	homemade chicken or veal stock, heated	1.1 L
	salt and pepper	

1 Heat butter in saucepan over medium heat. Sprinkle in flour and mix well. Cook 1 minute over low heat.

2 Incorporate half of stock and mix well using whisk. Continue cooking over low heat. When sauce begins to thicken, incorporate remaining stock. Season generously.

3 Cook sauce 30 minutes over very low heat. Stir occasionally during cooking.

4 Cover sauce with plastic wrap, touching surface. Refrigerate up to 3 days.

Cream of Beet Soup à la Serre
(4 servings)

2	large beets, cleaned	2
2 cups	white sauce, heated	500 mL
2 cups	chicken stock, heated	500 mL
½ cup	heavy cream	125 mL
	salt and pepper	
	cayenne pepper to taste	

Preheat oven to 375°F (190°C).

1 Place beets in oven and bake 2 hours or adjust time according to size. When cooked, peel off skin and purée.

2 Mix puréed beets with white sauce. Place in saucepan and incorporate chicken stock gradually. Whisk constantly. Season well with salt, pepper and cayenne pepper.

3 Add cream, mix and simmer soup 2 to 3 minutes over low heat. Serve.

Mixed Gumbo
(4 to 6 servings)

2 tbsp	butter	30 mL
¼ cup	diced carrots	50 mL
¼ cup	diced celery	50 mL
2	shallots, peeled and chopped	2
1 tsp	tarragon	5 mL
½ lb	fresh shrimp, peeled and deveined	225 g
½ cup	dry white wine	125 mL
3	tomatoes, peeled, seeded and chopped	3
1 tbsp	flour	15 mL
1	garlic clove, peeled, crushed and chopped	1
5 cups	chicken stock, heated	1.2 L
½ cup	rice, rinsed	125 mL
6 oz	frozen okra, sliced	170 g
	salt and pepper	
	cayenne pepper to taste	

1 Heat butter in large saucepan over medium heat. Add carrots, celery, shallots and tarragon. Cover and cook 3 minutes over low heat.

2 Increase heat to high and add shrimp. Cook 3 minutes uncovered. Pour in wine and continue cooking 1 minute. Remove shrimp from pan and set aside.

3 Add tomatoes to saucepan and season well. Cook 4 minutes over high heat. Mix in flour, garlic, chicken stock and rice. Season with salt, pepper and cayenne pepper.

4 Cook soup 10 minutes over low heat. Add okra and continue cooking 10 minutes.

5 When okra is cooked, add shrimp and simmer 2 minutes before serving.

Cold Tomato Soup
(4 servings)

1 tbsp	chopped fresh parsley	15 mL
1 tbsp	chopped fresh basil	15 mL
2	garlic cloves, blanched and puréed	2
2 tbsp	chopped red pimiento	30 mL
4	tomatoes, peeled, seeded and chopped	4
2	shallots, peeled and chopped	2
½	cucumber, peeled, seeded and diced	½
2 cups	chicken stock	500 mL
	salt and pepper	
	cayenne pepper to taste	

1 Place all ingredients, except chicken stock, in food processor. Blend briefly to combine.

2 Add chicken stock and season well. Blend very briefly then transfer soup to bowl.

3 Refrigerate 2 hours before serving. Accompany soup with croutons.

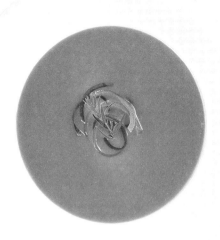

Portuguese Tomato and Rice Soup
(4 to 6 servings)

5	tomatoes, cored	5
2 tbsp	butter	30 mL
1	small onion, diced	1
1	carrot, pared and diced	1
½	celery stalk, diced	½
1	garlic clove, peeled and sliced	1
1 tbsp	basil	15 mL
⅓ cup	Italian Arborio rice, rinsed	75 mL
1 cup	chicken stock, heated	250 mL
	pinch of thyme	
	salt and pepper	
	pinch of sugar	
	fresh tarragon leaves	

1 Bring water to boil in large saucepan. Plunge tomatoes in boiling water just long enough to loosen skins. When cool enough to handle, peel skins and cut tomatoes in quarters. Squeeze out seeds and chop flesh coarsely.

2 Heat butter in saucepan over medium heat. Add onion, carrot, celery and garlic. Add seasonings, except fresh tarragon leaves and sugar, and mix well. Cook 4 minutes over low heat.

3 Stir in tomatoes, pinch of sugar and rice. Add chicken stock and season well. Cook soup 30 minutes over low heat.

4 Pass soup through food mill or purée in food processor. If soup is too thick, add more chicken stock to obtain desired consistency. Decorate portions with fresh tarragon leaves and julienned bell pepper.

Badoise Soup
(4 to 6 servings)

3 tbsp	butter	45 mL
2	Spanish onions, peeled and thinly sliced	2
1 tbsp	chopped fresh parsley	15 mL
3 tbsp	flour	45 mL
1 cup	dry white wine	250 mL
5 cups	chicken stock, heated	1.2 L
2	egg yolks	2
3 tbsp	heavy cream	45 mL
1 tbsp	chopped fresh chives	15 mL
	salt and pepper	
	few drops of lemon juice	

1 Heat butter in saucepan over medium heat. Add onions and parsley; cook 16 minutes over low heat.

2 Sprinkle in flour and mix well. Continue cooking 3 minutes. Pour in wine and chicken stock; mix again. Season well and cook soup 30 minutes over low heat. Do not cover.

3 Mix egg yolks with heavy cream. Add to soup and simmer 2 minutes. Do not let soup boil!

4 Add lemon juice, mix and serve at once with chopped chives.

Vichyssoise
(4 to 6 servings)

3	leeks, white part only	3
3 tbsp	butter	45 mL
2	onions, peeled and thinly sliced	2
4	large potatoes, peeled and sliced	4
3 cups	chicken stock, heated	750 mL
1 tbsp	chopped fresh basil	15 mL
1 tbsp	chopped fresh chervil	15 mL
1 cup	milk, heated	250 mL
½ cup	heavy cream	125 mL
	salt and pepper	
	cayenne pepper to taste	
	chopped fresh chives	

1 Slit leeks from top to bottom twice, leaving 1 in (2.5 cm) intact at base. Wash leeks under cold, running water to remove dirt and sand. Slice thinly.

2 Heat butter in large saucepan over medium heat. Add leeks and onions; season well. Cover and cook 10 minutes over low heat.

3 Add potatoes, chicken stock, basil and chervil. Continue cooking 20 minutes.

4 Pour soup into blender, then return soup to clean saucepan. Incorporate milk and cook 2 to 3 minutes over low heat.

5 Incorporate cream and let cool. Refrigerate soup 3 hours. Serve with chopped fresh chives.

Slit leeks from top to bottom twice, leaving 1 in (2.5 cm) intact at base. Wash leeks under cold, running water to remove dirt and sand. Slice thinly.

Heat butter in large saucepan over medium heat. Add leeks and onions; season well. Cover and cook 10 minutes over low heat.

Add potatoes, chicken stock, basil and chervil. Continue cooking 20 minutes.

Pour soup into blender, then return soup to clean saucepan. Incorporate milk and cook 2 to 3 minutes over low heat.

Chilled Sorrel Soup
(4 to 6 servings)

1 lb	fresh sorrel	450 g
1 cup	dry white wine	250 mL
5 cups	water	1.2 L
1 tbsp	sugar	15 mL
3	egg yolks	3
1 cup	heavy cream	250 mL
1	small cucumber, peeled, seeded and sliced	1
	salt and pepper	
	lemon wedges for garnish	

1 Wash sorrel well in plenty of cold water. Remove stems.

2 Chop sorrel coarsely and place in pot. Add wine and water; bring to boil. Cook 30 minutes over low heat. Add sugar, season well and continue cooking 8 minutes.

3 Mix egg yolks with cream. Incorporate 1 cup (250 mL) of sorrel cooking liquid into egg mixture. Pour contents into saucepan containing sorrel. Cook over very low heat for several minutes.

4 Remove from heat and transfer soup to bowl. Chill 4 hours in refrigerator. Serve with sliced cucumber and garnish with lemon wedges.

Quick Diced Vegetable Soup
(4 to 6 servings)

2 tbsp	butter	30 mL
1	onion, peeled and diced	1
1	celery stalk, diced	1
2	carrots, pared and diced	2
½	turnip, peeled and diced	½
1 tsp	basil	5 mL
½ tsp	thyme	2 mL
1 tsp	chervil	5 mL
6 cups	chicken or vegetable stock, heated	1.5 L
2	potatoes, peeled and diced	2
1 cup	frozen green peas	250 mL
1 cup	frozen corn	250 mL
	salt and pepper	

1 Heat butter in saucepan over medium heat. Add onion and celery. Cover and cook 4 minutes over low heat.

2 Add carrots, turnip and seasonings. Pour in stock and bring to boil. Cook 8 minutes over low heat. Do not cover.

3 Add potatoes and continue cooking 4 minutes.

4 Add peas and corn. Cook soup 10 minutes. Serve with grated cheese, if desired.

Creamy Hot Sorrel Soup
(4 to 6 servings)

3 tbsp	butter	45 mL
1	onion, peeled and sliced	1
½ lb	fresh sorrel, cleaned, stemmed and chopped	225 g
1 tbsp	chopped fresh basil	15 mL
1 tbsp	chopped fresh parsley	15 mL
2 cups	chicken stock, heated	500 mL
3	potatoes, peeled and sliced	3
1 cup	milk, heated	250 mL
1 cup	light cream, heated	250 mL
	salt and freshly ground pepper	

1 Heat butter in saucepan over medium heat. Add onion and sorrel; season well. Cover and cook 10 minutes over low heat.

2 Add seasonings, chicken stock and potatoes. Cook 18 minutes, uncovered, over low heat or until potatoes are cooked. Replenish liquid if needed.

3 When potatoes are cooked, incorporate milk and cream. Simmer 6 minutes and serve with small croutons.

Leek and Potato Soup
(4 to 6 servings)

4	large leeks, white part only	4
4 tbsp	butter	60 mL
5 cups	water	1.2 L
4	large potatoes, peeled and sliced	4
½ cup	heavy cream	125 mL
	salt and pepper	
	cayenne pepper to taste	

1 Slit leeks from top to bottom twice, leaving 1 in (2.5 cm) intact at base. Wash leeks under cold, running water to remove dirt and sand. Drain well and slice.

2 Heat butter in saucepan over medium heat. Add leeks and season well. Cover and cook 15 minutes over low heat.

3 Pour water into separate saucepan and add salt. Bring to boiling point. Add leeks and potatoes. Season with both peppers.

4 Cook soup 30 minutes over low heat, uncovered. Incorporate cream and serve.

Cream of Iceberg Lettuce
(4 servings)

4 tbsp	butter	60 mL
1	large head iceberg lettuce, washed, dried and thinly sliced	1
1	small onion, peeled and thinly sliced	1
½ tsp	thyme	2 mL
1 tbsp	chopped fresh parsley	15 mL
2 tbsp	chopped fresh basil	30 mL
1	bay leaf	1
5 tbsp	flour	75 mL
4 cups	chicken stock, heated	1 L
¼ cup	heavy cream (optional)	50 mL
	salt and pepper	
	cayenne pepper to taste	

1 Heat butter in saucepan over medium heat. Add lettuce, onion and all seasonings. Cover and cook 12 minutes over low heat.

2 Sprinkle in flour and mix well. Cook 1 minute, uncovered.

3 Pour in chicken stock and correct seasoning. Cook soup 25 minutes over low heat.

4 Pass soup through sieve into clean saucepan. Incorporate cream, if using, and simmer 3 minutes. Garnish with shredded red cabbage sautéed briefly in butter, if desired.

Borscht
(6 to 8 servings)

4	tomatoes, cored	4
1 tbsp	olive oil	15 mL
1	onion, peeled and chopped	1
2	garlic cloves, peeled and sliced	2
½	red cabbage, thinly sliced	½
4	fresh beets, peeled and cut in julienne	4
4	small potatoes, peeled and halved	4
5 cups	water	1.2 L
¼ cup	balsamic vinegar	50 mL
1 tsp	honey	5 mL
1	bouquet garni (thyme, bay leaf, sprigs of parsley and dill)	1
	salt and pepper	
	paprika to taste	

1 Plunge tomatoes in boiling water just long enough to loosen skins. When cool enough to handle, peel skins. Slice tomatoes in half, horizontally, and squeeze out seeds and juice. Set tomatoes aside.

2 Heat oil in large saucepan over medium heat. Add onion and garlic; cook 4 minutes.

3 Add all remaining ingredients. Cook soup 35 minutes, uncovered, over low heat.

4 Serve soup with chopped fresh dill and sour cream, if desired.

Cream of Fresh Mushroom
(4 servings)

4 tbsp	butter	60 mL
2	shallots, peeled and sliced	2
1 tbsp	basil	15 mL
¼ tsp	thyme	1 mL
1 tsp	tarragon	5 mL
1 lb	fresh mushrooms, cleaned and sliced	450 g
5 tbsp	flour	75 mL
4 cups	chicken stock, heated	1 L
½ cup	heavy cream	125 mL
4	fresh mushrooms, cleaned	4
	salt and freshly ground pepper	
	cayenne pepper to taste	

1 Heat butter in saucepan over medium heat. Add shallots and cook 2 minutes over low heat. Add seasonings and sliced mushrooms; cover and cook 12 minutes over low heat.

2 Sprinkle in flour and mix well. Cook 1 minute, uncovered. Incorporate chicken stock and season well. Cook soup 20 minutes over low heat uncovered.

3 Pass soup through food mill and incorporate cream.

4 Slice whole mushrooms and cook 2 minutes in small amount of lemony water. Drain very well and use to garnish soup.

Brussels Sprout and Potato Soup
(4 to 6 servings)

1 lb	fresh Brussels sprouts	450 g
3 tbsp	butter	45 mL
1	onion, peeled and sliced	1
½ tsp	thyme	2 mL
1 tbsp	chervil	15 mL
1 tbsp	basil	15 mL
3	potatoes, peeled and sliced	3
5 cups	chicken stock, heated	1.2 L
½ cup	heavy cream (optional)	125 mL
	salt and pepper	
	cayenne pepper to taste	

1 Remove outer leaves from Brussels sprouts and wash well. Using a paring knife, score an "X" on stems. This technique promotes even cooking.

2 Place Brussels sprouts in salted, boiling water. Cook 4 minutes. Drain well.

3 Heat butter in saucepan over medium heat. Add onion, cover and cook 5 minutes over low heat.

4 Add Brussels sprouts and all seasonings. Mix and add potatoes. Pour in chicken stock and season with salt and pepper. Bring to boil and cook soup 20 minutes over medium heat.

5 Drain vegetables, reserving stock, and purée in food processor. Add cooking liquid gradually, blending between additions, until desired consistency is reached.

6 Incorporate cream, if using, correct seasoning and serve.

Potage St. Germain
(4 to 6 servings)

1½ cups	dried split green peas	375 mL
1	onion, peeled and diced	1
1	large carrot, pared and diced	1
1	celery stalk, diced	1
2	garlic cloves, peeled	2
¼ tsp	thyme	1 mL
1 tbsp	chervil	15 mL
1 tbsp	tarragon	15 mL
1	bay leaf	1
1 cup	frozen green peas	250 mL
2 tbsp	chopped fresh chervil	30 mL
½ cup	heavy cream	125 mL
1½ cups	small croutons	375 mL
	salt and freshly ground pepper	
	cayenne pepper to taste	

1 Soak dried peas 8 hours in cold water. Drain well.

2 Place peas in pot and pour in enough water to cover. Bring to boil and cook 5 minutes; skim liquid. Drain peas and return to pot.

3 Add onion, carrot, celery and garlic to pot. Place dried herbs in piece of cheesecloth and secure with string. Add to pot. Pour in enough water to cover peas by 2 in (5 cm). Bring to boil and cook soup 40 minutes over low heat. Replenish liquid as needed to keep peas immersed.

4 Pass soup through food mill or purée in food processor. Place in clean saucepan.

5 Add frozen green peas, chervil and cream. Mix well and season with salt, pepper and cayenne pepper. Simmer over low heat until green peas are heated through. Serve with croutons.

Curried Cauliflower Soup
(4 to 6 servings)

1	small head cauliflower	1
4 tbsp	butter	60 mL
2	shallots, peeled and sliced	2
3 tbsp	Madras curry powder*	45 mL
4 tbsp	flour	60 mL
5 cups	chicken stock, heated	1.2 L
½ tsp	celery salt	2 mL
½ tsp	cumin	2 mL
	salt and pepper	

1 Remove green leaves from stem of cauliflower and core. Divide head into florets, wash well and drain.

2 Heat butter in large saucepan over medium heat. Add cauliflower and shallots; season well. Cover and cook 6 minutes over low heat.

3 Sprinkle in curry and mix well. Cook 4 minutes over low heat, uncovered.

4 Add flour, mix again, and continue cooking 2 minutes.

5 Pour in chicken stock and mix well. Add all seasonings and increase heat to high. Bring liquid to boil. Mix well and cook soup 20 minutes, uncovered, over low heat.

6 Pass soup through food mill. Add extra chicken stock if soup is too thick. Correct seasoning and serve with croutons.

*Madras curry powder is a hot variety. If not available, use regular curry powder.

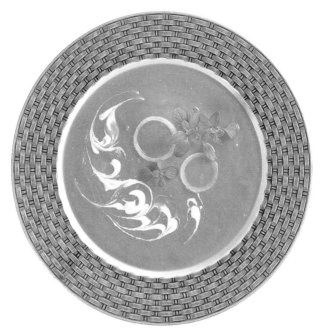

Provençale Country Soup
(4 to 6 servings)

3	potatoes, peeled and halved	3
3	tomatoes, peeled, seeded and coarsely chopped	3
6 cups	water	1.5 L
2 tbsp	olive oil	30 mL
2	onions, peeled and sliced	2
1	garlic clove, peeled and halved	1
	salt and pepper	
	toasted thick slices of French bread	

1 Place potatoes and tomatoes in large saucepan. Add water, season and bring to boil. Cook 1 hour over low heat.

2 Heat oil in sauté pan over medium heat. Add onions and cook 20 minutes over low heat. Be careful not to let onions burn.

3 Add 1 cup (250 mL) of potato/tomato liquid to onions in sauté pan. Cook 15 minutes over low heat.

4 Pass potatoes, tomatoes and contents of sauté pan through food mill or purée in food processor.

5 Ladle in enough soup liquid to obtain desired consistency. Season well.

6 Rub garlic over toasted bread. Place bread in bottom of soup bowl and cover with soup. Serve at once. Garnish with sour cream and oregano, if desired.

Cream Bretonne
(4 to 6 servings)

1½ cups	dried white peas or navy beans	375 mL
2 tbsp	butter	30 mL
2	leeks, white part only, cleaned and thinly sliced	2
2	onions, peeled and thinly sliced	2
1	sprig fresh thyme	1
2	sprigs fresh parsley	2
2	bay leaves	2
4	fresh basil leaves	4
2 tbsp	tomato paste	30 mL
¼ cup	heavy cream	50 mL
4	slices bacon, cooked and crumbled	4
	salt and pepper	
	cayenne pepper to taste	

1 Soak beans in cold water for 8 hours. Drain well.

2 Heat butter in large saucepan over medium heat. Add leeks and onions; cover and cook 6 minutes over low heat.

3 Add beans and all seasonings. Pour in enough cold water to cover beans by 2 in (5 cm). Bring to boil. Cook, partly covered, 2½ hours over low heat. Replenish liquid as needed to keep beans immersed.

4 Add tomato paste and mix well. Cook soup another 10 minutes.

5 Pass soup through sieve. Add cream and some hot broth if soup is too thick. Garnish with bacon and fresh fennel, if desired.

Soup for All Seasons
(6 servings)

3½ lb	cleaned chicken, tied	1.6 kg
1	onion, peeled and halved	1
1	celery stalk, halved	1
2	carrots, pared	2
1	sprig fresh thyme	1
2	sprigs fresh parsley	2
10 cups	water	2.5 L
3	leeks, white part only	3
¼ cup	butter	50 mL
5 tbsp	flour	75 mL
2 tbsp	chopped fresh tarragon	30 mL
	salt and pepper	
	cayenne pepper to taste	

1 Place chicken, onion, celery and carrots in large pot. Add thyme and parsley; season well. Pour in water, bring to boil and cook 4 minutes. Skim liquid. Cook 55 minutes over low heat, uncovered. Remove chicken when cooked, skin and dice meat. Strain cooking liquid and set aside.

2 Slit leeks from top to bottom twice, leaving 1 in (2.5 cm) intact at base. Wash leeks under cold, running water to remove dirt and sand. Drain and slice.

3 Heat butter in saucepan over medium heat. Add leeks and cook 8 minutes over low heat. Sprinkle in flour and mix well. Cook 1 minute.

4 Incorporate 5 cups (1.2 L) of reserved cooking liquid. Season well with salt, pepper and cayenne pepper. Cook 30 minutes over low heat.

5 Add chopped tarragon and desired amount of chicken. Simmer 2 minutes and serve.

Scallop and Mushroom Potage
(4 servings)

1 tbsp	butter	15 mL
1 lb	fresh scallops, cleaned	450 g
½ lb	fresh mushrooms, cleaned and sliced	225 g
4	green onions, chopped	4
1 cup	dry white wine	250 mL
3 cups	water	750 mL
½ tsp	fennel	2 mL
1 tbsp	chopped fresh parsley	15 mL
3 oz	Chinese noodles	90 g
	salt and pepper	
	cayenne pepper to taste	

1 Grease pot with butter. Add scallops, mushrooms and onions. Pour in wine and water. Add all seasonings. Cover with plastic wrap and bring to boiling point over medium heat.

2 As soon as liquid starts to boil, remove pot from heat. Using slotted spoon, transfer scallops to bowl and set aside.

3 Return pot to stove over medium heat. Continue cooking contents 10 minutes.

4 Add noodles and cook another 5 minutes.

5 When noodles are cooked, return scallops to pot. Simmer 3 minutes over low heat. Season and serve.

Curried Spinach Soup
(4 to 6 servings)

2	**bunches fresh spinach**	2
2 tbsp	**butter**	30 mL
1	**onion, peeled and chopped**	1
2	**shallots, peeled and chopped**	2
2 tbsp	**curry powder**	30 mL
1 tsp	**tumeric powder**	5 mL
2 tbsp	**flour**	30 mL
4 cups	**chicken stock, heated**	1 L
2 cups	**frozen green peas**	500 mL
½ cup	**light cream, heated**	125 mL
	salt and pepper	
	cayenne pepper to taste	

1 Remove stems from spinach. Wash spinach thoroughly in plenty of cold water. Repeat washing several times if necessary. Drain well and chop.

2 Heat butter in saucepan over medium heat. Add onion and shallots. Cook 4 minutes over low heat.

3 Sprinkle in curry and tumeric; mix well. Cook 2 minutes. Sprinkle in flour and mix well. Continue cooking 1 minute.

4 Add chopped spinach, season and mix well. Cover and cook 4 minutes over low heat.

5 Incorporate chicken stock and season well. Add peas and cook soup 8 to 10 minutes over medium heat.

6 Purée soup in food processor. Incorporate cream and correct seasoning. Serve soup warm or cold. Garnish with cooked spinach leaves, if desired.

Potage of Mixed Vegetables in Julienne
(4 to 6 servings)

3 tbsp	butter	45 mL
1	celery stalk, cut in julienne	1
2	green onions, cut in 1-in (2.5-cm) pieces	2
1	carrot, pared and cut in julienne	1
8	snow peas, cut in half lengthwise	8
1	red bell pepper, cut in julienne	1
1	large potato, peeled and cut in julienne	1
½	turnip, peeled and cut in julienne	½
6 cups	stock of your choice, heated	1.5 L
2	sprigs fresh parsley	2
1	sprig fresh tarragon	1
1	small sprig fresh rosemary	1
	salt and pepper	

1 Heat butter in saucepan over medium heat. Add all vegetables and season well. Cover and cook 8 minutes over low heat.

2 Pour in stock and add all seasonings. Bring to boil and cook 8 minutes over low heat. Do not cover.

3 Serve with toasted rye bread.

Old-Fashioned Cream of Chicken Soup
(4 to 6 servings)

¼ cup	butter	50 mL
1	small onion, peeled and finely chopped	1
1	leek, white part only, cleaned and sliced	1
½	celery stalk, diced	½
½ tsp	basil	2 mL
1 tsp	chopped fresh parsley	5 mL
¼ cup	flour	50 mL
5 cups	homemade chicken stock, heated (see p. 10)	1.2 L
1	egg yolk	1
½ cup	light cream	125 mL
½ cup	cooked rice	125 mL
1½ cups	cooked diced chicken	375 mL
	salt and pepper	

1 Heat butter in large saucepan over medium heat. Add vegetables and all seasonings. Cover and cook 8 minutes over low heat.

2 Sprinkle in flour and mix well. Cook 2 minutes, uncovered.

3 Incorporate chicken stock, mixing well with whisk. Season and cook soup 30 minutes over low heat, uncovered.

4 Mix egg yolk with cream; stir into soup. Add rice and chicken. Simmer soup 4 minutes over low heat. Do not let soup boil!

Potage Parisienne
(4 servings)

2	leeks, white part only, cleaned and sliced	2
4	potatoes, peeled	4
5 cups	chicken stock, heated	1.2 L
1 tbsp	chopped fresh basil	15 mL
1 tbsp	chopped fresh chervil	15 mL
3 tbsp	butter	45 mL
2 tsp	flour	10 mL
12	small slices French baguette	12
	salt and pepper	
	cayenne pepper to taste	
	grated Gruyère cheese	

1 Place leeks and potatoes in saucepan. Pour in chicken stock and add all seasonings. Cook over medium heat until potatoes are cooked.

2 Remove potatoes and pass through sieve. Set potatoes and soup broth aside separately.

3 Mix butter and flour together. Add to soup broth and whisk to incorporate. Add puréed potatoes and mix well. Season generously and simmer soup 4 minutes.

4 Meanwhile, place slices of bread in single layer on ovenproof tray. Top with grated Gruyère and put in oven set at broil until cheese melts.

5 Pour soup into bowls and garnish with wedges of bread.

Minestrone alla Milanese
(4 to 6 servings)

1 cup	dried white beans	250 mL
1 oz	salt pork, diced	30 g
1	onion, peeled and chopped	1
1	zucchini, diced	1
2	tomatoes, peeled, seeded and chopped	2
2	potatoes, peeled and diced	2
2 cups	cabbage, thinly sliced	500 mL
¼ cup	rice, rinsed	50 mL
2	garlic cloves, peeled, crushed and chopped	2
2 tbsp	chopped fresh basil	30 mL
½ cup	grated Parmesan cheese	125 mL
	salt and pepper	

1 Soak beans 8 hours in cold water. Drain.

2 Place beans in large saucepan. Add enough cold water to cover and season with salt. Bring to boil and skim water. Reduce heat to low and cook 1½ hours. Replenish liquid as needed to keep beans immersed.

3 Place salt pork in frying pan over medium heat. Add onion and zucchini; cook 7 minutes. Add remaining vegetables, season well and cook 4 minutes.

4 Add vegetables to beans in saucepan. Continue cooking 1 hour 10 minutes over low heat. Replenish liquid if needed to keep ingredients immersed.

5 Add rice, garlic and basil. Season generously and cook 20 minutes.

6 Add cheese, season and serve.

Place beans in large saucepan. Add enough cold water to cover and season with salt. Bring to boil and skim water.

Place salt pork in frying pan over medium heat. Add onion and zucchini; cook 7 minutes. Add remaining vegetables, season well and cook 4 minutes.

Add vegetables to beans in saucepan. Continue cooking 1 hour 10 minutes over low heat.

Add rice, garlic and basil. Season generously and cook 20 minutes.

Crabmeat Gumbo
(6 to 8 servings)

4 cups	beef stock	1 L
4 cups	water	1 L
1 lb	lean boneless blade roast	450 g
1	small veal bone, cracked in large pieces	1
4 tbsp	tomato paste	60 mL
1	sprig fresh thyme	1
2	sprigs fresh parsley	2
1	bay leaf	1
4 tbsp	butter	60 mL
1	Spanish onion, peeled and chopped	1
2 cups	frozen okra, halved	500 mL
4 tbsp	flour, browned lightly in oven	60 mL
1 lb	crabmeat	450 g
	salt and pepper	

1 Pour beef stock and water into pot. Add meat, veal bone and tomato paste. Add all seasonings and bring to boil. Skim liquid and cook 3 hours over low heat.

2 Remove meat and cut into small pieces. Strain cooking liquid. Set both aside separately.

3 Heat butter in large saucepan over medium heat. Add onion and cook 8 minutes over low heat. Add okra and continue cooking 4 minutes.

4 Sprinkle in browned flour and mix well. Incorporate cooking liquid and bring to boil. Season well.

5 Add meat and cook soup 30 minutes over low heat. Add crabmeat and continue cooking 4 minutes. Serve with rice.

Soup du Valais
(4 to 6 servings)

2	leeks, white part only, cleaned and sliced	2
1	onion, peeled and sliced	1
1	cauliflower, quartered	1
2 tbsp	butter	30 mL
2 tbsp	flour	30 mL
½ cup	rice, rinsed	125 mL
3 to 4	celery leaves	3 to 4
4 to 6	slices Havarti cheese	4 to 6
	salt and pepper	
	cayenne pepper to taste	

1 Place leeks in salted, boiling water and cook 10 minutes over medium heat. Add onion and cauliflower. Continue cooking 12 minutes. Remove vegetables from liquid and set aside.

2 Heat butter in saucepan over medium heat. Sprinkle in flour and mix well. Cook 1 minute.

3 Incorporate 4 cups (1 L) of cooking liquid from vegetables. Season and mix well. Add rice and celery leaves. Cook 20 minutes over low heat, uncovered.

4 Divide cauliflower into florets. Add to soup with leeks and onion. Simmer 3 minutes over low heat.

5 Place slice of cheese in each soup bowl. Add soup and serve.

Leek Soup with Gruyère Cheese
(4 to 6 servings)

2	leeks, white part only	2
3 tbsp	butter	45 mL
1	onion, peeled and sliced	1
4	potatoes, peeled and diced	4
2	sprigs fresh parsley	2
¼ tsp	thyme	1 mL
½ tsp	marjoram	2 mL
1	bay leaf	1
½ tsp	chervil	2 mL
6 cups	chicken stock, heated	1.5 L
1 cup	grated Gruyère cheese	250 mL
	salt and pepper	
	pinch of nutmeg	

1 Slit leeks from top to bottom twice, leaving 1 in (2.5 cm) intact at base. Wash leeks under cold, running water to remove dirt and sand. Slice leeks.

2 Heat butter in large saucepan over medium heat. Add leeks and onion. Cover and cook 12 minutes over low heat. Stir twice during cooking.

3 Add potatoes. Place all seasonings, except nutmeg, in piece of cheesecloth and secure with string. Add to saucepan.

4 Pour in chicken stock and season with nutmeg. Cook soup 30 minutes over low heat, uncovered.

5 Divide grated cheese among soup bowls. Pour in soup and serve.

Garlic Lover's Potage
(4 to 6 servings)

24	garlic cloves, peeled	24
6 cups	water	1.5 L
¼ cup	butter	50 mL
2 cups	croutons	500 mL
4	egg yolks	4
1 cup	grated Gruyère cheese	250 mL
	salt and pepper	
	cayenne pepper to taste	

1 Place garlic in saucepan and add water. Season with salt, pepper and cayenne pepper. Cook 16 minutes over medium heat.

2 Using slotted spoon, remove garlic cloves. Purée garlic in mortar, then return to saucepan containing water.

3 Heat butter in frying pan over medium heat. Add croutons and sauté 2 to 3 minutes. Divide croutons among soup bowls.

4 Beat egg yolks together in bowl. Incorporate 1 cup (250 mL) of hot soup liquid to egg yolks. Mix very well, then pour egg yolks into saucepan containing soup. Whisk to incorporate. Simmer soup 4 minutes over very low heat.

5 Serve soup over croutons and top with grated cheese. Garnish with croutons, if desired.

Cock-a-Leekie
(4 to 6 servings)

BROTH:

2 lb	veal bones	900 g
2 lb	chicken bones, cleaned	900 g
10 cups	water	2.5 L
1	leek, white part only, cleaned	1
2	carrots, pared and halved	2
2	celery stalks, diced	2
1	sprig fresh thyme	1
2	sprigs fresh parsley	2
4	fresh basil leaves	4
2	bay leaves	2
12	black peppercorns	12
2	cloves	2
	salt and pepper	

1 Place bones in large saucepan and add water. Bring to boil and cook 8 minutes; skim liquid.

2 Add remaining ingredients and cook, partly covered, 2 hours over low heat.

3 Strain contents of pan and reserve broth.

SOUP:

3	leeks, white part only	3
2 tbsp	butter	30 mL
1 cup	pitted prunes	250 mL
1	whole chicken breast, cooked, skinned and sliced	1
	salt and pepper	
	chopped fresh parsley	

1 Slit leeks from top to bottom twice, leaving 1 in (2.5 cm) intact at base. Wash leeks under cold, running water to remove dirt and sand. Cook leeks in boiling water for 15 minutes. Drain well and slice thinly.

2 Heat butter in saucepan over medium heat. Add leeks, prunes and chicken. Cover and simmer 4 minutes.

3 Incorporate broth and correct seasoning. Simmer 2 minutes, sprinkle with chopped parsley and serve.

Fresh Fish Soup with Mushrooms
(4 servings)

2 tbsp	butter	30 mL
½ lb	fresh mushrooms, cleaned and sliced	225 g
1	shallot, peeled and chopped	1
3	fresh sole fillets, rinsed	3
½ cup	dry white wine	125 mL
½ cup	water	125 mL
1	onion, peeled and chopped	1
2 cups	clam juice	500 mL
1	egg yolk	1
1 cup	light cream	250 mL
	salt and pepper	
	cayenne pepper to taste	
	pinch of paprika	
	chopped fresh parsley	

1 Grease frying pan with 1 tbsp (15 mL) of butter. Add mushrooms, shallot and fish. Season well, pour in wine and water. Cover with sheet of waxed paper and bring to boil over medium-low heat.

2 Remove fish from pan and set aside. Continue cooking liquid 5 minutes over low heat.

3 Heat remaining butter in saucepan over medium heat. Add onion and cook 6 minutes.

4 Pour in clam juice, cooking liquid from fish and mushrooms. Mix egg yolk with cream; stir into soup. Season with cayenne pepper and paprika.

5 Dice fish and add to soup. Correct seasoning, add parsley and simmer 3 minutes. Serve.

Velvety Cream of Avocado
(4 to 6 servings)

1 lb	fresh spinach, washed well	450 g
4 tbsp	butter	60 mL
4 tbsp	flour	60 mL
2 cups	milk, heated	500 mL
2 cups	chicken stock, heated	500 mL
¼ cup	heavy cream	50 mL
2	ripe avocados, peeled and flesh puréed	2
1 tbsp	chopped fresh basil	15 mL
	salt and pepper	
	cayenne pepper to taste	
	few drops of lemon juice	

1 Cook spinach in small amount of salted, boiling water for 6 minutes. Transfer spinach to sieve and squeeze out excess water by pressing leaves with back side of spoon. Place spinach in food processor and purée.

2 Heat butter in saucepan over medium heat. Add flour and cook 1 minute. Pour in milk and mix well. Add chicken stock and mix well. Season and cook 3 minutes over medium heat.

3 Mix in puréed spinach. Continue cooking 6 minutes.

4 Pass soup through food mill into bowl. Incorporate cream and puréed avocado. Sprinkle in fresh basil and correct seasoning.

5 Add few drops of lemon juice to prevent soup from discoloring. Serve chilled.

Old-Fashioned Asparagus Soup
(4 to 6 servings)

1 lb	fresh asparagus	450 g
3 tbsp	butter	45 mL
2 tbsp	chopped fresh tarragon	30 mL
4 tbsp	butter	60 mL
4 tbsp	flour	60 mL
2 cups	milk, heated	500 mL
2 cups	stock of your choice, heated	500 mL
¼ cup	heavy cream	50 mL
	juice of ½ lemon	
	salt and pepper	
	cayenne pepper to taste	

1 Clean asparagus and pare if necessary. Snap off ends and discard. Dice remaining stalks.

2 Heat 3 tbsp (45 mL) butter in saucepan over medium heat. Add asparagus, tarragon and lemon juice. Season with salt, pepper and cayenne pepper. Cover and cook 20 minutes over low heat.

3 Heat remaining butter in separate saucepan over medium heat. Sprinkle in flour and mix well. Cook 1 minute.

4 Incorporate milk using whisk, then incorporate stock. Season well and cook 15 minutes over low heat.

5 Add cooked asparagus and juices in pan to cooking soup. Season well and pass through food mill.

6 Incorporate cream, correct seasoning and serve.

Cream of Seafood
(4 servings)

1 lb	fresh shrimp, peeled and deveined	450 g
5 tbsp	butter	75 mL
2	large shallots, peeled and chopped	2
1	red bell pepper, diced	1
¼ tsp	fennel seeds	1 mL
1 tsp	chervil	5 mL
⅓ cup	flour	75 mL
2 cups	clam juice	500 mL
3 cups	milk, heated	750 mL
	salt and freshly ground pepper	
	pinch of paprika	
	pinch of cayenne pepper	

1 Reserve 6 whole shrimp and chop remaining.

2 Heat butter in saucepan over medium heat. Add chopped shrimp, shallots, bell pepper and all seasonings. Cover and cook 8 minutes over low heat.

3 Sprinkle in flour and mix well. Cook 1 minute, uncovered. Incorporate clam juice and hot milk. Correct seasoning and cook soup 20 minutes over low heat.

4 Pass soup through food mill into clean saucepan. Simmer over low heat.

5 Dice reserved shrimp. Cook 1 minute in lemony water. Add diced shrimp to soup, simmer 1 minute and serve.

Lobster Gazpacho
(6 servings)

2	leeks, white part only	2
2	celery stalks, cut in short julienne	2
1	cucumber, seeded and cut in short julienne with peel	1
4	large tomatoes, peeled, seeded and diced	4
1	cucumber, peeled, seeded and diced	1
4	sprigs fresh chervil, chopped	4
1	red bell pepper, diced	1
3	garlic cloves, peeled, crushed and chopped	3
1 tbsp	white vinegar	15 mL
2 cups	light cream, heated	500 mL
1	large cooked lobster, meat diced	1
	salt and pepper	
	cayenne pepper	

1 Slit leeks from top to bottom twice, leaving 1 in (2.5 cm) intact at base. Wash leeks under cold, running water to remove dirt and sand. Slice.

2 Place leeks and celery in saucepan. Add water to cover and cook 10 minutes over medium heat. Reduce heat to low and add julienned cucumber. Cook 2 minutes. Drain vegetables well and set aside.

3 Place tomatoes, diced cucumber, chervil, bell pepper and garlic in food processor. Blend briefly.

4 Transfer mixture to saucepan and add 1 cup (250 mL) water and vinegar. Season with salt, pepper and cayenne pepper. Cover and cook 5 minutes over medium-low heat.

5 Increase heat and incorporate cream. Simmer liquid for 3 minutes.

6 Remove saucepan from stove. Add julienned vegetables and lobster meat. Chill at least 4 hours before serving.

Chicken Creole Gumbo
(6 to 8 servings)

3 tbsp	butter	45 mL
1	onion, peeled and chopped	1
1	celery stalk, diced	1
1	leek, white part only, cleaned and sliced	1
1	green bell pepper, diced	1
1	red bell pepper, diced	1
½ cup	diced Virginia ham	125 mL
1	chicken leg, skinned, boned and diced	1
5 cups	homemade chicken stock, heated (see page 10)	1.2 L
¼ cup	rice, rinsed	50 mL
8	fresh okra	8
2	tomatoes, peeled, seeded and diced	2
	salt and pepper	

1 Heat butter in saucepan over medium heat. Add onion, celery, leek and bell peppers. Cover and cook 8 minutes over low heat. Stir in ham and chicken. Cook 4 minutes, uncovered.

2 Pour in chicken stock and season well. Cook soup 20 minutes over low heat, uncovered. Add rice and continue cooking 15 minutes.

3 Add okra and tomatoes. Cook another 5 minutes. Serve gumbo with garlic bread.

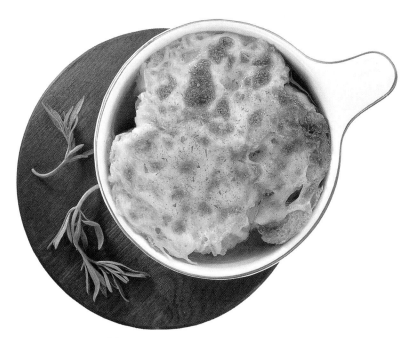

Basic Onion Soup au Gratin
(4 to 6 servings)

3 tbsp	butter	45 mL
3	Spanish onions, peeled and sliced	3
1 cup	dry white wine	250 mL
7 cups	beef stock, heated	1.8 L
1	sprig fresh thyme	1
1	sprig fresh basil	1
1	sprig fresh parsley	1
2	bay leaves	2
1½ cups	grated Gruyère cheese	375 mL
	thick slices of French bread	
	salt and pepper	

1 Remove crust from bread and trim slices to fit soup bowls. Toast and set aside.

2 Heat butter in sauté pan over medium heat. Add onions and cook 35 minutes over low heat. Stir occasionally during cooking. Onions should brown nicely (without burning) and become soft.

3 Pour in wine. Continue cooking 6 minutes, uncovered.

4 Pour in beef stock. Place fresh herbs and bay leaves in piece of cheesecloth and secure with string. Drop into soup. Season well with salt and pepper. Cook soup 30 minutes over low heat.

5 Place 1 tbsp (15 mL) of cheese in bottom of each ovenproof soup bowl. Arrange bowls on ovenproof tray. Add soup and position toasted bread. Top with cheese.

6 Broil in middle of preheated oven about 15 minutes or until golden brown. Serve.

Basic Tomato Soup
(4 to 6 servings)

5 cups	water	1.2 L
6	tomatoes, cored	6
¼ cup	butter	50 mL
1	Spanish onion, peeled and thinly sliced	1
1	garlic clove, peeled and sliced	1
5 tbsp	flour	75 mL
1	sprig fresh thyme	1
2	sprigs fresh parsley	2
2	sprigs fresh basil	2
1	bay leaf	1
1 tsp	sugar	5 mL
	salt and pepper	
	sour cream (for decoration)	
	chopped fresh chives	

1 Bring water to boil in large saucepan. Plunge tomatoes in boiling water just long enough to loosen skins. When cool enough to handle, peel skins and cut tomatoes in quarters. Do not seed.

2 Return quartered tomatoes to boiling water. Season with salt and pepper and cook 15 minutes over low heat.

3 Meanwhile, heat butter in saucepan over medium heat. Add onion and garlic; cook 15 minutes over low heat.

4 Sprinkle in flour and mix well. Cook 2 minutes over low heat.

5 Measure 2 cups (500 mL) of tomato stock. Pour into saucepan containing onion. Mix well and cook 1 minute.

6 Pour onion mixture into saucepan containing remaining stock and tomatoes. Mix very well. Add herbs, bay leaf and sugar and season well. Cook soup 30 minutes over low heat.

7 Pass soup through sieve before serving. Garnish with sour cream and chopped fresh chives.

Using a teaspoon, place 3 drops of sour cream on the surface of each tomato soup.

Position the blade of a knife in front of the first drop of sour cream.

Run the tip of the blade smoothly through the 3 drops to form the heart-shaped design.

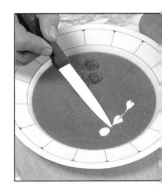

Garnish soup with croutons and chopped chives.

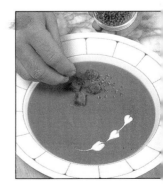

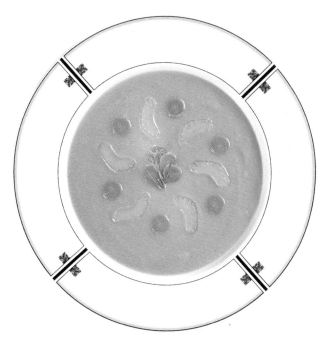

Purée of White Beans
(4 to 6 servings)

1½ cups	dried navy beans	375 mL
1	onion, peeled and studded with 1 clove	1
1	garlic clove, peeled and sliced	1
1	carrot, pared and diced	1
½	celery stalk, diced	½
1 tbsp	chopped fresh parsley	15 mL
1 tbsp	chopped fresh basil	15 mL
¼ tsp	marjoram	1 mL
1 cup	chicken stock	250 mL
	salt and pepper	

1 Soak beans in water overnight. Drain and transfer beans to large saucepan. Pour in fresh water to cover and bring to boil. Cook 5 minutes and skim liquid.

2 Drain beans and return to same saucepan. Add onion, garlic, carrot, celery and all seasonings. Pour in fresh water to cover and bring to boil. Cook beans, partly covered, 2½ to 3 hours over low heat. Replenish water as needed to keep beans immersed.

3 When cooked, pass soup through food mill into bowl. Start by adding 1 cup (250 mL) chicken stock. If soup is still too thick, add more chicken stock to obtain desired consistency. Serve with French bread.

Fresh Okra and Tomato Soup
(4 to 6 servings)

3 lb	chicken bones, cleaned	1.4 kg
10 cups	water	2.5 L
2	leeks, white part only	2
2	onions, peeled and cut in eighths	2
2	celery stalks, chopped	2
3	tomatoes, peeled, seeded and chopped	3
2 cups	sliced cooked fresh okra	500 mL
1½ cups	cooked rice	375 mL
2	tomatoes, peeled, seeded and diced	2
1	celery stalk, diced	1
	salt and pepper	
	cayenne pepper to taste	

1 Place chicken bones in large saucepan and add water. Bring to boil and cook 6 minutes; skim liquid.

2 Slit leeks from top to bottom twice, leaving 1 in (2.5 cm) intact at base. Wash leeks under cold, running water to remove dirt and sand.

3 Add whole leeks, onions, chopped celery and chopped tomatoes to saucepan. Season well with salt, pepper and cayenne pepper. Cook 1 hour over low heat.

4 Remove chicken bones and discard. Strain contents of saucepan through sieve into clean saucepan.

5 Add okra, rice, remaining tomatoes and celery to broth. Correct seasoning and cook 5 minutes over low heat. Serve.

Brandy Shrimp Soup with Vegetables
(4 servings)

3 tbsp	butter	45 mL
¼ cup	diced carrots	50 mL
¼ cup	diced celery	50 mL
2	shallots, peeled and diced	2
1 lb	fresh shrimp, peeled and deveined	450 g
3 tbsp	brandy	45 mL
½ cup	dry white wine	125 mL
4 cups	white sauce, heated (see p. 14)	1 L
	salt and freshly ground pepper	
	pinch of paprika	
	pinch of cayenne pepper	
	chopped fresh parsley	

1 Heat butter in frying pan over medium heat. Add diced vegetables and cook 5 minutes over high heat. Add shrimp, season and continue cooking 4 minutes.

2 Pour in brandy and flambé. Add wine and continue cooking 2 minutes.

3 Reserve one shrimp per serving; set aside. Transfer remaining contents of frying pan to food processor. Blend to purée.

4 Place white sauce in clean saucepan and incorporate puréed shrimp and vegetable mixture. Season with salt, pepper, paprika and cayenne pepper; mix well.

5 Simmer soup 5 minutes over low heat. Garnish each serving with one whole shrimp and chopped parsley.

Cream of Watercress
(4 servings)

4 tbsp	butter	60 mL
2	bunches fresh watercress, cleaned and chopped	2
1	shallot, peeled and chopped	1
5 tbsp	flour	75 mL
5 cups	chicken stock, heated	1.2 L
¼ cup	heavy cream (optional)	50 mL
	salt and pepper	
	cayenne pepper to taste	

1 Heat butter in saucepan over medium heat. Add watercress, shallot and season well. Cover and cook 15 minutes over low heat.

2 Sprinkle in flour and mix well. Cook 1 minute, uncovered. Incorporate chicken stock using whisk and correct seasoning. Cook 25 minutes over low heat. Do not cover.

3 Pass soup through food mill and incorporate cream, if using. Season and serve. Garnish with chives and sliced green onions, if desired.

Beer Soup
(4 to 6 servings)

¼ cup	butter	50 mL
1	Spanish onion, peeled and thinly sliced	1
1 tbsp	chopped fresh parsley	15 mL
1 tbsp	chopped fresh basil	15 mL
½ cup	flour	125 mL
5 cups	beer, at room temperature	1.2 L
2	egg yolks	2
½ cup	heavy cream	125 mL
	pinch of sugar	
	salt and pepper	

1 Heat butter in saucepan over medium heat. Add onion and herbs; cover and cook 30 minutes over low heat. Stir 3 times during cooking.

2 Sprinkle in flour and mix well. Cook 1 minute.

3 Pour in beer and mix well. Add sugar and season with salt and pepper. Bring to boil. Cook soup 30 minutes over low heat, uncovered.

4 Mix egg yolks with cream. Reduce heat under saucepan to low. Stir egg yolk mixture into soup and simmer 2 minutes. Serve.

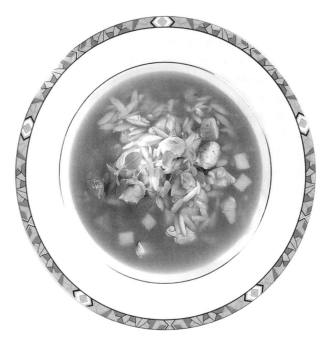

Chicken Orzo Soup
(4 to 6 servings)

1	leek, white part only	1
3½ lb	cleaned chicken, tied	1.6 kg
1	onion, peeled	1
2	carrots, pared	2
12 cups	water	3 L
2 tbsp	butter	30 mL
2	shallots, peeled and chopped	2
1½ cups	orzo	375 mL
1	cucumber, peeled, seeded and diced	1
	salt and pepper	

1 Slit leek from top to bottom twice, leaving 1 in (2.5 cm) intact at base. Wash leek under cold, running water to remove dirt and sand.

2 Place chicken, leek, onion and carrots in large pot. Pour in water, season well and bring to boil. Cook 4 minutes and skim liquid. Cook 55 minutes over low heat, uncovered. Remove chicken when cooked, skin and dice meat. Strain cooking liquid and set aside.

3 Heat butter in saucepan over medium heat. Add shallots and orzo. Cook 3 minutes. Incorporate 3 cups (750 mL) of reserved cooking liquid. Cook 12 to 15 minutes.

4 Add cucumber and desired amount of diced chicken. Season well, mix and simmer 5 minutes.

5 If soup is too thick, add more cooking liquid to obtain desired consistency.

Curried Oyster Soup
(4 servings)

3 tbsp	butter	45 mL
1	onion, peeled and finely chopped	1
½	celery stalk, finely diced	½
1 tbsp	curry powder	15 mL
1 tsp	chopped fresh parsley	5 mL
¼ tsp	thyme	1 mL
½ cup	white breadcrumbs	125 mL
2 cups	milk, heated	500 mL
36	fresh shucked oysters	36
3 tbsp	dry white wine	45 mL
½ cup	heavy cream (optional)	125 mL
	salt and pepper	
	cayenne pepper and paprika to taste	
	chopped fresh chives	

1 Heat butter in saucepan over medium heat. Add onion and celery; cover and cook 4 minutes over low heat.

2 Stir in curry, parsley and thyme. Cover and cook 6 minutes over low heat.

3 Mix in breadcrumbs, then pour in milk. Mix well. Season with salt, pepper, cayenne pepper and paprika. Cook 10 minutes over low heat. Do not cover.

4 Place juice from oyster shells and wine in separate saucepan. Bring to simmer over low heat. Add oysters and poach 3 to 4 minutes. Outside edges of oysters will curl up when cooked.

5 Remove cooked oysters and set aside. Pass remaining liquid through sieve. Set aside.

6 Pass milk mixture through food mill into clean saucepan. Incorporate oyster liquid, mix and cook 2 minutes.

7 Add oysters and simmer 2 minutes. Add cream if using, sprinkle with chives and serve.

Cream of Turnip
(4 to 6 servings)

3 tbsp	butter	45 mL
1	onion, peeled and sliced	1
1	garlic clove, peeled and sliced	1
1	small turnip, peeled and sliced	1
4	potatoes, peeled and sliced	4
1 tsp	basil	5 mL
1 tsp	tarragon	5 mL
¼ tsp	thyme	1 mL
6 cups	chicken stock, heated	1.5 L
¼ cup	heavy cream (optional)	50 mL
	salt and pepper	

1 Heat butter in saucepan over medium heat. Add onion and garlic; cook 4 minutes over low heat.

2 Add turnip, potatoes, salt and pepper; mix well. Add remaining seasonings and pour in chicken stock; bring to boil. Cook 30 minutes over low heat, uncovered.

3 Pass soup through food mill or purée in food processor. Incorporate cream, if using, and serve.

European Chicken Soup

(4 to 6 servings)

BROTH:

4 lb	chicken, cleaned	1.8 kg
16 cups	water	4 L
1	leek, white part only, cleaned and cut in 3	1
1	onion, halved	1
2	celery stalks, chopped	2
1	sprig fresh thyme	1
2	sprigs fresh parsley	2
2	bay leaves	2
1 tsp	marjoram	5 mL
	salt and pepper	

1 Place all ingredients in large pot. Bring to boil and cook 90 minutes over low heat.

2 Remove chicken from pot, leaving liquid in pot. Discard skin and trim off all meat. Dice meat and set aside.

3 Return chicken carcass to pot with liquid. Cook 1 hour over low heat. Strain liquid through sieve lined with cheesecloth. Set chicken broth aside.

SOUP:

2	leeks, white part only	2
¼ cup	butter	50 mL
1	onion, peeled and chopped	1
¼ cup	flour	50 mL
	salt and pepper	

1 Slit leeks from top to bottom twice, leaving 1 in (2.5 cm) intact at base. Wash leeks under cold, running water to remove dirt and sand. Slice leeks.

2 Heat butter in large saucepan over medium heat. Add leeks and onion; cover and cook 12 minutes over low heat.

3 Sprinkle in flour and mix well. Incorporate 4 cups (1 L) of chicken broth. Mix very well and season to taste. Cook 20 minutes over low heat.

4 Pass soup through food mill into clean saucepan. Add diced chicken and simmer soup 5 minutes before serving.

Soup à la Soubise
(4 to 6 servings)

1 lb	green onions	450 g
5 tbsp	butter	75 mL
½ tsp	sugar	2 mL
5 tbsp	flour	75 mL
4 cups	stock of your choice, heated	1 L
¼ cup	heavy cream	50 mL
	salt and pepper	
	cayenne pepper to taste	
	fresh chervil	

1 Cut off and discard green tops from onions. Place whole onions in pot with salted, boiling water. Cook 20 minutes over medium heat. Drain well.

2 Heat butter in saucepan over medium heat. Add cooked onions and sugar. Cover and cook 12 minutes over low heat.

3 Sprinkle in flour and mix well. Cook 1 minute over low heat. Incorporate stock and season well. Cook soup 18 minutes over low heat.

4 Pass soup through food mill. Incorporate cream and chervil. Serve.

Lyonnaise Soup au Gratin

(serves 6)

BROTH:

2 lb	veal bones, cut in half	900 g
2 lb	chicken bones, cleaned	900 g
10 cups	water	2.5 L
1	leek, cleaned and halved	1
2	carrots, pared and halved	2
1	celery stalk, halved	1
2	onions, halved	2
1	red banana pepper, halved	1
1	sprig fresh thyme	1
2	sprigs fresh parsley	2
½ cup	fresh basil leaves	125 mL
2	bay leaves	2
15	black peppercorns	15
2	cloves	2
	salt and pepper	

1 Place bones in large pot and add water. Bring to boil and cook 10 minutes; skim liquid.

2 Add remaining ingredients. Cook 1½ hours over low heat. Strain liquid through sieve lined with cheesecloth. Set aside.

SOUP:

3 tbsp	butter	45 mL
2	Spanish onions, peeled and thinly sliced	2
1 tsp	sugar	5 mL
6	thick slices bread	6
1½ cups	grated Gruyère cheese	375 mL
	salt and pepper	

1 Heat butter in sauté pan over medium heat. Add onions, cover and cook 15 minutes over low heat. Remove cover and continue cooking 30 minutes over low heat. Stir frequently to prevent burning.

2 Sprinkle in sugar, mix and cook 3 minutes.

3 Pour in 6 cups (1.5 L) of broth and season well. If soup is too thick, add more broth to obtain desired consistency. Simmer soup several minutes.

4 Toast slices of bread lightly on both sides. Ladle soup into ovenproof bowls. Top with bread and cover with grated cheese.

5 Broil 5 minutes in oven. Serve.

Vegetable Baked Soup au Gratin
(4 servings)

2 tbsp	butter	30 mL
1	onion, peeled and thinly sliced	1
1	Boston lettuce, washed and sliced	1
1 tbsp	chopped fresh parsley	15 mL
1 tbsp	chopped fresh basil	15 mL
2 cups	frozen green peas	500 mL
5 cups	chicken stock, heated	1.2 L
4	slices stale French bread, sized to fit soup bowls	4
1 cup	grated Swiss cheese	250 mL
	salt and pepper	

1 Heat butter in saucepan over medium heat. Add onion, cover and cook 2 minutes over low heat. Add lettuce and seasonings. Cover and cook another 8 minutes.

2 Add peas and pour in chicken stock. Season well and cook soup 10 minutes, uncovered, over medium heat.

3 Pour soup into ovenproof bowls and top with slice of bread. Sprinkle with grated cheese and broil 6 minutes in oven until golden brown. Serve.

Creamy Tarragon Tomato Soup
(4 to 6 servings)

5 tbsp	butter	75 mL
4 tbsp	flour	60 mL
4 cups	milk, heated	1 L
4	tomatoes, peeled, seeded and diced	4
½	celery stalk, diced	½
2	shallots, peeled and chopped	2
1 tsp	sugar	5 mL
2 tbsp	chopped fresh tarragon	30 mL
	salt and pepper	

1 Heat 4 tbsp (60 mL) butter in saucepan over medium heat. Sprinkle in flour and mix well. Cook 1 minute.

2 Incorporate milk using whisk. Season and cook 12 minutes over low heat. Stir frequently during cooking.

3 Heat remaining butter in separate saucepan over medium heat. Add tomatoes, celery, shallots, sugar and tarragon. Season well and cook 8 minutes over high heat.

4 Transfer vegetable mixture to food processor. Blend to purée.

5 Using whisk, incorporate vegetable purée to milk in saucepan. Cook soup 6 minutes over low heat. Serve.

Zucchini, Tomato and Mushroom Soup
(4 to 6 servings)

3 tbsp	butter	45 mL
2	large potatoes, peeled and cut in julienne	2
2	zucchini, cut in julienne	2
½ lb	fresh mushrooms, cleaned and sliced	225 g
3	tomatoes, peeled, seeded and chopped	3
3	green onions, chopped	3
1 tbsp	chopped fresh basil	15 mL
6 cups	chicken stock, heated	1.5 L
4 tsp	sour cream	20 mL
	salt and pepper	
	cayenne pepper to taste	

1 Heat butter in saucepan over medium heat. Add potatoes and zucchini; season well. Cover and cook 6 minutes.

2 Add remaining vegetables and all seasonings. Cover and continue cooking 8 minutes.

3 Pour in chicken stock and cook 4 minutes over low heat. Do not cover.

4 Serve with sour cream.

Pistachio Nut Soup

(4 servings)

4 tbsp	butter	60 mL
5 tbsp	flour	75 mL
4 cups	chicken stock, heated	1 L
1 cup	pistachio nuts	250 mL
¼ cup	butter	50 mL
¼ cup	heavy cream	50 mL
1 tbsp	chopped fresh chives	15 mL
	salt and pepper	
	cayenne pepper to taste	

1 Heat 4 tbsp (60 mL) butter in saucepan over medium heat. Sprinkle in flour and mix well. Cook 1 minute over low heat.

2 Incorporate chicken stock using whisk and season well. Cook soup 20 minutes over low heat.

3 Purée nuts with ¼ cup (50 mL) butter. Incorporate into soup, then mix in cream. Simmer 5 minutes over very low heat.

4 Sprinkle with chives and serve.

Shrimp and Potato Chowder
(4 to 6 servings)

2 cups	clam juice	500 mL
2 cups	water	500 mL
2	sprigs fresh parsley	2
1	sprig fresh thyme	1
½ tsp	fennel seeds	2 mL
½ tsp	tarragon	2 mL
1 lb	fresh shrimp, peeled and deveined	450 g
2	carrots, pared and diced	2
3	medium size potatoes, peeled and diced	3
4 tbsp	butter	60 mL
4 tbsp	flour	60 mL
	salt and pepper	
	pinch of cayenne pepper	

1 Pour clam juice and water into pot. Place all seasonings in piece of cheesecloth and secure with string. Add to pot.

2 Add shrimp and vegetables. Bring slowly to boil. Remove cooked shrimp and set aside.

3 Continue cooking vegetables 12 minutes or until completely cooked. Season with salt and pepper. Strain cooking liquid, reserving vegetables separately.

4 Heat butter in saucepan over medium heat. Sprinkle in flour and mix well. Cook 1 minute.

5 Incorporate strained cooking liquid, mixing well with whisk. Cook 6 minutes over low heat.

6 Add shrimp and reserved vegetables to soup. Simmer over low heat for 1 to 2 minutes or until reheated. Sprinkle with chopped parsley or fresh fennel before serving, if desired.

Potage à la Crécy
(4 to 6 servings)

6 tbsp	butter	90 mL
1 lb	spring carrots, thinly sliced	450 g
2	shallots, peeled and sliced	2
1 tbsp	chopped fresh chervil	15 mL
½ tsp	sugar	2 mL
5 cups	chicken stock, heated	1.2 L
½ cup	rice, rinsed	125 mL
	salt and pepper	

1 Heat 4 tbsp (60 mL) butter in saucepan over medium heat. Add carrots, shallots and chervil. Cover and cook 12 minutes over low heat.

2 Stir in sugar and cook 5 minutes, uncovered.

3 Season well and pour in chicken stock. Add rice and cook soup 20 minutes over medium heat.

4 Pass soup through food mill or purée in blender. Stir in remaining butter and serve.

Heat 4 tbsp (60 mL) butter in saucepan over medium heat. Add carrots, shallots and chervil. Cover and cook 12 minutes over low heat.

Stir in sugar and cook 5 minutes, uncovered.

Season well and pour in chicken stock. Add rice and cook soup 20 minutes over medium heat.

Pass soup through food mill or purée in blender. Stir in remaining butter and serve.

Oyster Velouté
(4 to 6 servings)

⅓ cup	butter	75 mL
1	shallot, peeled and chopped	1
½ lb	fresh mushrooms, cleaned and sliced	225 g
4 tbsp	flour	60 mL
2 cups	clam juice	500 mL
1½ cups	water	375 mL
½ cup	dry white wine	125 mL
24	shucked fresh oysters	24
½ cup	heavy cream	125 mL
	salt and pepper	
	cayenne pepper to taste	
	pinch of paprika	
	chopped fresh chives	

1 Heat butter in saucepan over medium heat. Add shallot and mushrooms. Season and cook 5 minutes.

2 Sprinkle in flour and mix well. Cook 2 minutes.

3 Incorporate clam juice and water; season well. Cook sauce 8 minutes over low heat. Add cayenne pepper and paprika.

4 Pour wine in another saucepan over medium heat. Bring to boil and cook 2 minutes. Add oysters and reduce heat to low; poach 2 minutes.

5 Remove oysters and set aside. Continue cooking liquid remaining in pan 3 minutes.

6 Incorporate liquid to velouté sauce, mixing well with whisk. Stir in heavy cream and add oysters. Simmer 2 minutes over low heat.

7 Garnish with fresh chives and serve.

Lentil Frankfurter Soup
(4 to 6 servings)

1½ cups	dried lentils, rinsed	375 mL
2 tbsp	butter	30 mL
1	onion, peeled and chopped	1
1	celery stalk, diced	1
1	carrot, pared and diced	1
2	garlic cloves, peeled and sliced	2
6 cups	beef stock, heated	1.5 L
2	potatoes, peeled and grated	2
4	frankfurters, sliced	4
	salt and pepper	
	cayenne pepper to taste	

1 Place lentils in pot and cover with cold water. Bring to boil and cook 5 minutes; drain lentils.

2 Heat butter in large saucepan over medium heat. Add vegetables and garlic; cook 4 minutes over low heat.

3 Add lentils and season well. Pour in beef stock and bring to boil. Reduce heat to low and cook soup 75 minutes. Replenish liquid as needed to keep lentils immersed.

4 Add potatoes and frankfurters. Continue cooking 12 minutes. If soup is too thick, thin to desired consistency with more stock.

Cream of Celery Soup
(4 to 6 servings)

5	celery stalks, diced	5
1	onion, peeled and chopped	1
1	sprig fresh thyme	1
2	sprigs fresh parsley	2
3	fresh basil leaves	3
1	bay leaf	1
6 cups	water	1.5 L
5 tbsp	butter	75 mL
2	celery stalks from the celery heart	2
5 tbsp	flour	75 mL
¼ cup	heavy cream (optional)	50 mL
	salt and pepper	

1 Place diced celery stalks in pot with onion and seasonings. Add water and bring to boil. Cook 1 hour over low heat. Pass liquid through sieve lined with cheesecloth. Set aside.

2 Heat butter in saucepan over medium heat. Dice remaining celery stalks finely and add to saucepan. Cook 8 minutes over low heat. Sprinkle in flour and mix well. Cook 1 minute.

3 Incorporate celery broth and mix well. Correct seasoning and cook soup 20 minutes over low heat. Stir in cream, if using, and serve.

Mussel Chowder

(4 servings)

4½ lb	fresh mussels, bearded and cleaned	2 kg
4	shallots, peeled and finely chopped	4
1 tbsp	chopped fresh parsley	15 mL
4 tbsp	butter	60 mL
1	sprig fresh thyme	1
1 cup	dry white wine	250 mL
2 cups	clam juice, heated	500 mL
3 tbsp	flour	45 mL
1 cup	light cream, heated	250 mL
	salt and pepper	
	pinch of paprika	

1 Place mussels, shallots, parsley and 1 tbsp (15 mL) of butter in large pot. Add thyme and wine. Cover and cook 6 minutes over medium heat or until mussels open.

2 Remove mussels from pot, discarding any that did not open.

3 Strain cooking liquid from mussels and return to pot. Add clam juice and cook 6 minutes over medium heat.

4 Heat remaining butter in saucepan over medium heat. Sprinkle in flour and mix well. Cook 1 minute over low heat.

5 Incorporate reduced cooking liquid to saucepan. Mix very well with whisk. Cook sauce 6 minutes over low heat. Pour in cream, mix and season well.

6 Remove mussels from shells and add to soup. Simmer just to reheat, then serve with a pinch of paprika.

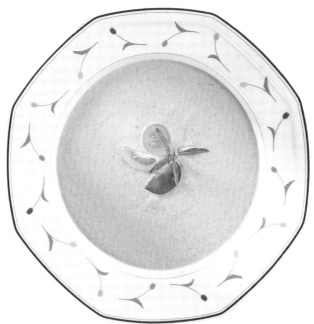

Potage Verte
(4 to 6 servings)

¾ lb	fresh sorrel	350 g
4 tbsp	butter	60 mL
1	onion, peeled and sliced	1
5 tbsp	flour	75 mL
5 cups	chicken stock, heated	1.2 L
½ cup	heavy cream (optional)	125 mL
	salt and pepper	
	cayenne pepper to taste	

1 Trim thick stalks from sorrel. Wash sorrel thoroughly in plenty of cold water. Repeat washing several times, if necessary. Drain well and chop.

2 Heat butter in large saucepan over medium heat. Add onion, cover and cook 3 minutes over low heat.

3 Add sorrel and season with salt, pepper and cayenne pepper. Cover and cook 10 minutes over low heat.

4 Sprinkle in flour and mix well. Incorporate chicken stock and correct seasoning. Bring to boil and cook soup 30 minutes over low heat.

5 Pass soup through food mill or purée in food processor. Incorporate cream, if using, and serve.

Tomato Blender Soup
(4 servings)

2 tbsp	butter	30 mL
½	onion, peeled and finely chopped	½
1	garlic clove, peeled, crushed and chopped	1
5	tomatoes, peeled, seeded and chopped	5
1 tbsp	chopped fresh basil	15 mL
3 tbsp	flour	45 mL
2 cups	chicken stock, heated	500 mL
½ tsp	sugar	2 mL
	salt and pepper	

1 Heat butter in saucepan over medium heat. Add onion, cover and cook 4 minutes over low heat.

2 Add garlic, tomatoes, basil and season well. Cook 5 minutes over high heat, uncovered.

3 Sprinkle in flour and mix well. Cook 1 minute over low heat. Incorporate stock and bring to boil. Add sugar and cook soup 12 minutes over low heat.

4 Pour mixture into food processor and purée to desired consistency. Add more liquid if necessary. Serve with crusty buns.

Lentil Soup with Tomatoes
(4 to 6 servings)

1 tbsp	olive oil	15 mL
2	small smoked pork cutlets, diced	2
1	onion, peeled and diced	1
½	celery stalk, diced	½
1	garlic clove, peeled, crushed and chopped	1
3	tomatoes, peeled, seeded and chopped	3
1½ cups	dried lentils, rinsed	375 mL
6 cups	chicken stock, heated	1.5 L
2	sprigs fresh parsley	2
1	bay leaf	1
¼ tsp	thyme	1 mL
1 tbsp	chopped fresh basil	15 mL
½ tsp	marjoram	2 mL
	salt and pepper	

1 Heat oil in saucepan over medium heat. Add pork, onion, celery and garlic. Cook 4 minutes over low heat.

2 Add tomatoes, season well and continue cooking 4 minutes.

3 Stir in lentils and chicken stock.

4 Place all seasonings in piece of cheesecloth and secure with string. Add to soup.

5 Bring to boil and cook soup 1½ hours over low heat. Replenish liquid as needed to keep lentils immersed.

6 Serve with croutons, if desired.

Heat oil in saucepan over medium heat. Add pork, onion, celery and garlic. Cook 4 minutes over low heat.

Add tomatoes, season well and continue cooking 4 minutes.

Stir in lentils and chicken stock.

Place all seasonings in piece of cheesecloth and secure with string. Add to soup.

Potage Duxelles
(4 to 6 servings)

¼ cup	butter	50 mL
3	shallots, peeled and chopped	3
1	garlic clove, peeled and sliced	1
1 lb	fresh mushrooms, cleaned and chopped	450 g
4 tbsp	flour	60 mL
4 cups	chicken stock, heated	1 L
½ cup	heavy cream (optional)	125 mL
	few drops of lemon juice	
	salt and pepper	
	cayenne pepper and paprika to taste	

1 Heat butter in saucepan over medium heat. Add shallots and garlic; cover and cook 3 minutes over low heat.

2 Add mushrooms and lemon juice. Cover and continue cooking 12 minutes over low heat.

3 Sprinkle in flour and mix well. Cook 1 minute, uncovered.

4 Pour in chicken stock and mix very well. Season with salt, pepper, cayenne pepper and paprika. Cook soup 20 minutes over low heat. Do not cover.

5 Pass soup through food mill into clean saucepan. Add cream, if using, simmer 4 minutes and serve.

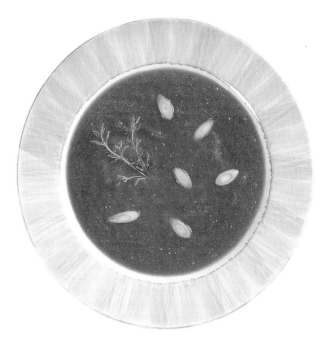

Cold Vegetable Soup
(4 to 6 servings)

3	tomatoes, peeled, seeded and chopped	3
1	cucumber, peeled, seeded and sliced	1
1	yellow bell pepper, sliced	1
1	red bell pepper, sliced	1
2	green onions, sliced	2
1	garlic clove, peeled and sliced	1
2	apples, cored, peeled and sliced	2
1 tbsp	tomato paste	15 mL
¼ tsp	thyme	1 mL
2 tbsp	chopped fresh tarragon	30 mL
2 tbsp	olive oil	30 mL
4 cups	chicken stock	1 L
	salt and pepper	

1 Place vegetables, garlic and apples in food processor. Blend to incorporate.

2 Pour mixture into bowl and add remaining ingredients. Mix well and correct seasoning.

3 Chill for at least 3 hours or overnight. Serve cold.

Purée of Celeriac
(4 to 6 servings)

1 lb	celeriac, peeled and sliced in fine julienne	450 g
2 tbsp	butter	30 mL
1	onion, peeled and sliced	1
2 tbsp	chopped fresh basil	30 mL
3	large potatoes, peeled and sliced	3
4½ cups	chicken stock, heated	1.1 L
¼ cup	heavy cream	50 mL
	salt and pepper	
	garlic bread	

1 Place celeriac in salted, boiling water and cook 12 minutes. Drain well.

2 Heat butter in saucepan over medium heat. Add celeriac and onion. Cover and cook 8 minutes over low heat.

3 Add basil, potatoes and chicken stock. Season well and bring to boil. Cook 30 minutes over low heat, uncovered.

4 Pass soup through food mill into bowl. Incorporate cream and serve soup with garlic bread.

French Country Beef and Vegetable Soup

(6 to 8 servings)

3 lb	boneless blade roast	1.4 kg
10 cups	water	2.5 L
4	leeks, white part only	4
2	celery stalks, cut in two	2
8	green onions	8
4	carrots, pared	4
4	potatoes, peeled	4
1	turnip, peeled and quartered	1
1	cabbage, quartered	1
1	garlic clove	1
	several sprigs of fresh herbs (thyme, parsley, rosemary, tarragon, etc.)	
	salt and pepper	

1 Place meat in large pot and add water. Bring to boil and cook for 10 minutes; skim liquid.

2 Slit leeks from top to bottom twice, leaving 1 in (2.5 cm) intact at base. Wash leeks under cold, running water to remove dirt and sand. Tie leeks together.

3 Tie celery stalks and green onions in separate bunches. Add tied leeks, celery and green onions to soup. Add remaining vegetables and garlic.

4 Place fresh herbs in piece of cheesecloth and secure with string. Add to soup. Season very well with salt and pepper.

5 Cook soup 3 hours over very low heat. Monitor vegetables and remove as soon as cooked. Untie and cover cooked vegetables with some of the cooking liquid to keep warm.

6 When meat is cooked, cut into pieces and place portions in each soup bowl. Add assortment of vegetables and cover with broth.

Chilled Split Green Pea Soup
(6 to 8 servings)

1 ½ cups	dried green split peas	375 mL
8 cups	water	2 L
1	onion, peeled and chopped	1
1	celery stalk, diced	1
1	carrot, pared and sliced	1
1	garlic clove, peeled	1
1 cup	heavy cream	250 mL
	salt and freshly ground pepper	
	cayenne pepper to taste	
	chopped fresh chives	

1 Soak peas 8 hours in cold water. Drain well.

2 Place peas in large pot with 8 cups (2 L) water. Bring to boil and cook 3 minutes; skim liquid.

3 Add vegetables, garlic and season well. Bring to boil and cook soup, partly covered, 40 minutes over low heat. Replenish liquid as needed to keep peas immersed.

4 Pass soup through food mill or purée in food processor. Incor-. porate cream and refrigerate 4 hours before serving. Sprinkle portions with fresh chives just before serving.

Lentil Soup with Smoked Ham
(4 to 6 servings)

1 ½ cups	dried lentils	375 mL
1	onion, peeled and chopped	1
1	carrot, peeled and diced	1
½	celery stalk, diced	½
2	garlic cloves, peeled	2
2	sprigs fresh parsley	2
1	sprig fresh thyme	1
1 tsp	basil	5 mL
1 tsp	marjoram	5 mL
1	bay leaf	1
12	black peppercorns	12
1 tsp	rosemary	5 mL
6 oz	smoked ham, diced	170 g
2 tbsp	butter	30 mL
1 ½ cups	chicken stock, heated	375 mL
	salt and pepper	

1 Place lentils in pot and cover with water. Bring to boil and cook 5 minutes. Drain lentils.

2 Return lentils to pot, add vegetables and ham. Place all seasonings in piece of cheesecloth and secure with string. Add to pot and cover with fresh water. Bring to boil.

3 Cook soup, partly covered, 1½ hours over low heat. Replenish water as needed to keep ingredients immersed.

4 When cooked, stir in butter. Add chicken stock to obtain desired consistency. Serve with fresh bread.

Basic Cream of Leek

(4 servings)

2	large leeks, white part only	2
5 tbsp	butter	75 mL
2	large shallots, peeled and sliced	2
½ tsp	chopped bay leaves	2 mL
1 tsp	basil	5 mL
¼ tsp	thyme	1 mL
⅓ cup	flour	75 mL
5 cups	milk, heated	1.2 L
	salt and freshly ground pepper	
	cayenne pepper to taste	
	chopped fresh chives	

1 Slit leeks from top to bottom twice, leaving 1 in (2.5 cm) intact at base. Wash leeks under cold, running water to remove dirt and sand. Drain well and slice.

2 Heat butter in saucepan over medium heat. Add leeks, shallots and all seasonings, except chives. Mix well, cover and cook 20 minutes over low heat.

3 Sprinkle in flour and mix well. Cook 1 minute, uncovered. Incorporate milk and season with salt, pepper and cayenne pepper. Cook soup 20 minutes over low heat. Stir 2 to 3 times during cooking.

4 Pass soup through food mill. Serve with fresh chives and croutons, if desired.

Black-Eyed Pea Soup
(4 to 6 servings)

1 ½ cups	dried black-eyed peas	375 mL
1	onion, peeled and chopped	1
1	carrot, pared and diced	1
½	celery stalk, diced	½
2	sprigs fresh parsley	2
¼ tsp	thyme	1 mL
1 tsp	basil	5 mL
½ tsp	marjoram	2 mL
1	bay leaf	1
1 tsp	chervil	5 mL
12	black peppercorns	12
2 cups	chicken stock, heated	500 mL
	salt and pepper	
	cayenne pepper to taste	

1 Soak black-eyed peas in cold water for 8 hours. Drain.

2 Place peas in pot and cover with fresh water. Bring to boil and cook 5 minutes; skim liquid. Drain peas.

3 Return peas to pot and cover with fresh water. Add vegetables. Place all seasonings in piece of cheesecloth and secure with string. Add to pot. Bring to boil.

4 Cook peas, partly covered, 2½ to 3 hours over low heat. Replenish with water as needed to keep ingredients immersed.

5 When cooked, pass soup through food mill or purée in food processor. Add chicken stock to obtain desired consistency. Serve.

Manhattan Clam Chowder
(4 to 6 servings)

40	fresh clams, cleaned	40
2 cups	water	500 mL
3 tbsp	butter	45 mL
1	onion, peeled and finely chopped	1
1	celery stalk, diced	1
1	yellow bell pepper, diced	1
1	green bell pepper, diced	1
1	leek, white part only, cleaned and sliced	1
3	tomatoes, peeled, seeded and chopped	3
2	garlic cloves, peeled, crushed and chopped	2
2	large potatoes, peeled and diced	2
2 cups	clam juice	500 mL
	several sprigs of fresh herbs	
	salt and pepper	
	few drops of Tabasco sauce	

1 Place clams in pot with water. Cover and cook 6 minutes or until shells open. Stir once or twice during cooking. Discard any unopened shells.

2 Remove clams from pot and remove from shells. Set aside. Strain cooking liquid and set aside separately.

3 Heat butter in saucepan over medium heat. Add onion, celery, bell peppers and leek. Season and cook 8 minutes.

4 Add tomatoes and garlic. Increase heat to high and cook 4 minutes. Stir in potatoes, reserved cooking liquid and clam juice. Season with salt and pepper.

5 Place fresh herbs in piece of cheesecloth and secure with string. Add to saucepan. Cook soup 30 minutes over low heat, uncovered.

6 Chop clams; add to soup. Sprinkle in Tabasco sauce, simmer 3 minutes, and serve.

Broccoli Potage
(4 to 6 servings)

3	small heads broccoli	3
4 tbsp	butter	60 mL
1	onion, peeled and thinly sliced	1
1	shallot, peeled and thinly sliced	1
4 tbsp	flour	60 mL
5 cups	chicken stock, heated	1.2 L
1	sprig fresh parsley	1
¼ tsp	thyme	1 mL
1	bay leaf	1
1 tsp	basil	5 mL
1 cup	milk, heated	250 mL
	salt and pepper	

1 Divide broccoli into florets; soak 15 minutes in cold water. Drain and pat dry.

2 Heat butter in saucepan over medium heat. Add onion and shallot; cook 3 minutes.

3 Add broccoli and season well. Cover and cook 12 minutes over low heat.

4 Sprinkle in flour and mix well. Cook 1 minute, uncovered.

5 Add chicken stock and all seasonings. Cook soup 30 minutes over low heat, uncovered.

6 Pass soup through food mill or purée in food processor. Return to saucepan and incorporate milk. Cook 2 minutes over high heat.

7 Serve soup garnished with fresh basil and tomato slices, if desired.

Minestrone Soup
(serves 6 to 8)

2 tbsp	olive oil	30 mL
1	celery stalk, diced	1
1	leek, white part only, cleaned and sliced	1
1	onion, peeled and diced	1
2	carrots, pared and diced	2
¼	head cabbage, sliced	¼
2	garlic cloves, peeled	2
3	tomatoes, peeled, seeded and chopped	3
2 tbsp	tomato paste	30 mL
6 cups	homemade beef stock (see p. 12)	1.5 L
½ cup	frozen green peas	125 mL
1 cup	short pieces of spaghetti	250 mL
	salt and freshly ground pepper	
	grated Parmesan cheese	

1 Heat oil in large saucepan over medium heat. Add celery, leek, onion, carrots and cabbage. Season well. Cover and cook 10 minutes over low heat.

2 Add garlic and tomatoes. Cook 4 minutes, uncovered.

3 Mix in tomato paste and beef stock. Season well and cook soup 1 hour over low heat, uncovered.

4 Stir in peas and spaghetti. Continue cooking 15 minutes. Season with pepper and serve with grated Parmesan cheese.

Cream of Fresh Chervil
(4 servings)

5 tbsp	butter	75 mL
2	large bunches fresh chervil, washed and chopped	2
5 tbsp	flour	75 mL
5 cups	chicken stock, heated	1.2 L
½ cup	heavy cream	125 mL
	salt and freshly ground pepper	

1 Heat butter in saucepan over medium heat. Add chervil and season well. Cover and cook 12 minutes over low heat.

2 Sprinkle in flour and mix well. Cook 1 minute over low heat. Incorporate stock using whisk. Correct seasoning and cook soup 30 minutes over low heat. Do not cover.

3 Pass soup through food mill. Incorporate cream and serve.

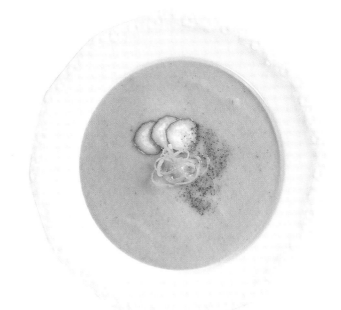

Cold Potato and Cucumber Soup
(4 to 6 servings)

3	potatoes, peeled and sliced	3
3	cucumbers, peeled and seeded	3
2 tbsp	butter	30 mL
1	onion, peeled and sliced	1
1 tbsp	chopped fresh basil	15 mL
1 tbsp	chopped fresh parsley	15 mL
½ tsp	grated lemon rind	2 mL
4 cups	chicken stock, heated	1 L
½ cup	heavy cream	125 mL
	salt and pepper	

1 Place sliced potatoes in bowl of cold water; set aside.

2 With one cucumber, make 16 balls using melon baller. Blanch cucumber balls in boiling water for 1 to 2 minutes. Drain and set aside.

3 Slice remaining cucumbers and set aside.

4 Heat butter in saucepan over medium heat. Add onion and herbs; cook 3 minutes.

5 Drain potatoes and pat dry. Add potatoes and sliced cucumbers to saucepan. Sprinkle in lemon rind, season and cook 2 minutes.

6 Pour in chicken stock, mix and cook soup 20 minutes over low heat.

7 Pass soup through food mill into bowl. Incorporate cream and refrigerate 2 hours. Stir in cucumber balls before serving.

Chilled Avocado Soup with Lemon
(4 servings)

2	ripe avocados, peeled and sliced	2
2 tbsp	chopped green onions	30 mL
1 tsp	chopped fresh parsley	5 mL
1 tsp	curry powder	5 mL
3 cups	chicken stock, heated	750 mL
2 tbsp	plain yogurt	30 mL
	few drops of Tabasco sauce	
	few drops of lemon juice	
	salt and pepper	
	sour cream (optional)	

1 Place all ingredients, except chicken stock, yogurt and sour cream in food processor. Blend 1 minute.

2 Transfer mixture to bowl and incorporate hot chicken stock. Mix well and stir in yogurt. Correct seasoning.

3 Chill soup 3 hours. Serve decorated with sour cream, if desired.

Index